Writing 9

Gary Snyder's Books:

Earth House Hold
Myths & Texts
Riprap & Cold Mountain Poems
Regarding Wave
The Back Country

GARY SNYDER

Six Sections from
Mountains and Rivers without End
Plus One

Four Seasons Foundation

San Francisco: 1970

Six of these sections were first published in *Caterpillar,
City Lights Journal, Origin* and *Wild Dog;* "The Blue Sky"
was also published in a limited edition by the Phoenix Book Shop

Library of Congress Catalog Card No.: 78-114627
Standard Book No.: 0-87704-003-6

Cover design: Indian petroglyph found on the lower terraces of
the Pyramid Range, Nevada (from Robert F. Heizer and Martin
A. Baumhoff: *Prehistoric Rock Art of Nevada and Eastern
California*, fig. 115 e)

The Writing Series is edited by Donald Allen and published
by Four Seasons Foundation, 1815 Jones Street, San Francisco,
California 94109
Distributed by Book People, 2010 Seventh Street, Berkeley,
California 94710

Contents

Bubbs Creek Haircut

for Locke McCorkle

High ceilingd and the double mirrors, the
        calendar a splendid alpine scene—scab barber—
in stained white barber gown, alone, sat down, old man
A summer fog gray San Francisco day
I walked right in.   on Howard street
              haircut a dollar twenty-five.
Just clip it close as it will go.
     "now why you want your hair cut back like that."
     —well I'm going to the Sierras for a while
Bubbs Creek and on across to upper Kern.
             he wriggled clippers,
"Well I been up there, I built the cabin
     up at Cedar Grove. In nineteen five."
             old haircut smell

Next door, Goodwill.
         where I came out.
A search for sweater, and a stroll
        in the board & concrete room of
     unfixed junk downstair—
All emblems of the past—too close—
     heaped up in chilly dust and bare bulb glare
Of tables, wheelchairs, battered trunks & wheels
& pots that boiled up coffee nineteen ten, *things*
Swimming on their own & finally freed
           from human need. Or?
    waiting a final flicker of desire
To tote them out once more.   Some freakish use.
The Master of the limbo drag-legged watches
            making prices

1

                    to the people seldom buy
The sag-asst rocker has to make it now. Alone.

                         A few weeks later drove with Locke
          down San Joaquin, us barefoot in the heat
          stopping for beer & melon on the way
                              the Giant Orange,
          rubber shreds of cast truck retreads on the pebble
          shoulders, highway ninety-nine.
                              Sierras marked by cumulus
                              in the east.
          car coughing in the groves,   six thousand feet;
          down to Kings River Canyon; camped at Cedar Grove.
                         hard granite canyon walls that
                         leave no scree

Once tried a haircut at the Barber College too—
Sat half an hour before they told me
                    white men use the other side.
Goodwill, St. Vincent de Paul,
                    Salvation Army, up the coast
For mackinaws and boots and heavy socks
               —Seattle has the best for logger gear
Once found a pair of good tricouni
               at the under-the-public-market store,
               Mark Tobey's scene,
                    torn down I hear—
& Filson jacket with a birdblood stain.

A. G. & me got winter clothes for almost nothing
               at Lake Union, telling the old gal
               we was on our way
To work the winter out up in B. C.
                              hitch-hiking home the
Green hat got a ride (of that more later)

                              2

hiking up Bubbs Creek saw the trail crew tent
in a scraggly grove of creekside lodgepole pine
                    talked to the guy, he says
"If you see McCool on the other trailcrew over there
tell him Moorehead says to go to hell."
late snow that summer. Crossing the scarred bare
                    shed of Forester Pass
        the winding rock-braced switchbacks
dive in snowbanks, we climb on where
                    pack trains have to dig or wait.
a half iced-over lake, twelve thousand feet
                    its sterile boulder bank
but filled with leaping trout:
                    reflections wobble in the
mingling circles always spreading out
            the crazy web of wavelets makes sense
            seen from high above.
the realm of fallen rock.
a deva world of sorts—it's high
                it is a view that few men see, a point
            bare sunlight
            on the spaces
empty sky
                moulding to fit the shape of what ice left
of fire-thrust, or of tilted, twisted, faulted
                    cast-out from this lava belly globe.

The boulder in my mind's eye is a chair.
                    . . . why was the man drag legg'd?
King of Hell
            or is it a paradise of sorts, thus freed
From acting out the function some
                        creator/carpenter
Thrust on a thing to think he made, himself,

3

an object always "chair"
                    Sinister ritual histories.
            is the Mountain God a gimp?
"le Roi Boeuf" and the ritual limp?
                            Good   Will?

Daughter of mountains, stoopd
            moon breast Parvati
    mountain thunder speaks
    hair tingling static as the lightning lashes
    is neither word of love or wisdom;
    though this be danger: hence thee fear.
                    Some flowing girl
    whose slippery dance
    entrances Shiva
                    —the valley spirit/ Anahita,
                            Sarasvati,
    dark and female gate of all the world
    water that cuts back quartzflake sand
                    Soft is the dance that melts the
    mat-haired mountain sitter
                    to leap in fire
    & make of sand a tree
            of tree a board, of board (ideas!)
            somebody's rocking chair.
    a room of empty sun of peaks and ridges
            beautiful spirits,
                            rocking lotus throne:
    a universe of junk, all left alone.

The hat I always take on mountains:
When we came back down through Oregon
                    (three years before)
At nightfall in the Siskiyou few cars pass

4

A big truck stopped a hundred yards above
         "Siskiyou Stoneware" on the side
The driver said
He recognized my old green hat.
I'd had a ride
         with him two years before
A whole state north
         when hitching down to Portland
                  from Warm Springs.
Allen in the rear on straw
  forgot salami   and we went on south
  all night—in many cars—to Berkeley in the dawn.

     upper Kern River country now after nine days walk
     it finally rain.
        we ran on that other trail crew
     setting up new camp in the drizzly pine
     cussing & slapping bugs, 4 days from road,
     we saw McCool, & he said tell that Moorehead
           KISS MY ASS
     we squatted smoking by the fire.
        "I'll never get a green hat now"
     the foreman says   fifty mosquitoes sitting on the brim
                  they must like green.
    & two more days of thundershower and cold
        (on Whitney hair on end
        hail stinging barelegs in the blast of wind
        but yodel off the summit echoes clean)

     all this came after:
Purity of the mountains and goodwills.
The diamond drill of racing icemelt waters
        and bumming trucks & watching

Buildings raze
        the garbage acres burning at the Bay
        the girl who was the skid-row
Cripple's daughter—

                out of the memory of smoking pine
The lotion and the spittoon glitter rises
Chair turns and in the double mirror waver
The old man cranks me down and cracks a chuckle

            "your Bubbs Creek haircut, boy."

                        20.IV.60

6

The Elwha River

I was a girl waiting by the roadside for my boyfriend to come
in his car. I was pregnant, I should have been going to high
school. I walked up the road when he didn't come, over a bridge;
I saw a sleeping man. I came to the Elwha River—grade
school—classes—I went and sat down with the children.
The teacher was young and sad-looking, homely; she assigned
us an essay:
"What I Just Did."

"I was waiting for my boyfriend by the Elwha bridge. The bridge
was redwood, a fresh bridge with inner bark still clinging on
some logs—it smelled good. There was a man there sleeping
under redwood trees. He had a box of flies by his head; he was
on the ground. I crossed the Elwha River by a meadow; it had
a flat stony prong between two river forks . . ."

Thinking this would please the teacher. We handed all the
papers in, and got them back—mine was C minus. The children
then went home; the teacher came to me and said "I don't
like you."
"Why?"
—"Because I used to be a whore."

The Elwha River, I explained, is a real river, but not the river I
described. Where I had just walked was real but for the dream
river—actually the Elwha doesn't fork at that point.

As I write this I must remind myself that there is another Elwha,
the actual Olympic peninsula river, which is not the river I took
pains to recollect as real in the dream.

There are no redwoods north of southern
Curry County, Oregon.

21.X.1958

II

Marble hollow-ground hunting knife;

pigleather tobacco pouch
left on the ground at Whiskey Bend along
the Elwha, 1950—

Sewing kit. Blown off the cot beside me
on the boatdeck by a sudden wind
South China Sea;

A black beret Joanne had given me for my birthday
left in some
Kawaramachi bar.

Swiss army knife stole from my pants
at Juhu Beach outside Bombay,
a fine italic pen,

Theodora, Kitty-chan,
bottle of wine got broke.
things left on the sand.

Lost things.

III

Elwha, from its source. Threadwhite falls
out of snow-tunnel mouths with
cold mist-breath

saddles of deep snow on the ridges—

      o wise stream—o living flow
   o milky confluence, bank cutter
         alder toppler
         make meander,
swampy acres   elk churned mud

    The big Douglas fir in this valley.
    Nobly groovd bark, it adapts: where Sitka spruce
    cannot.
        Redwood and sequoia
    resisting and enduring, as against adaptation;
    one mind.

    Trail crew foreman says they finally got wise
to making trails low on the outside, so water
can run off good—before they were worried because
packstock always walks the outside of the trail
because they don't want to bump their loads on rocks
or trees.   "punching out all the way from N Fork
over Low Divide & clear back here, this punchin gets
mighty old"

Puncheon slab saw cut *wowed*

"They got rip-cut chains now maybe different rakers
   this here punchin gets old"

    About 12:30 come to Whiskey Bend.
    That lowland smell.

                          21.VIII.1964

Night Highway Ninety-nine

*. . . only the very poor, or eccentric, can surround themselves
with shapes of elegance (soon to be demolished) in which they
are forced by poverty to move with leisurely grace. We remain
alert so as not to get run down, but it turns out you only have
to hop a few feet, to one side, and the whole huge machinery
rolls by, not seeing you at all.*

—LEW WELCH

I

We're on our way
            man
        out of town
     go hitching down
     that highway ninety-nine

Too cold and rainy to go out on the Sound
Sitting in Ferndale drinking coffee
Baxter in black, been to a funeral
Raymond in Bellingham—Helena Hotel—
Can't go to Mexico with that weak heart
Well you boys can go south. I stay here.
Fix up a shack—get a part-time job—
            (he disappeared later
             maybe found in the river)
In Ferndale & Bellingham
Went out on trailcrews
Glacier and Marblemount
There we part.

                    tiny men with moustaches
                    driving ox-teams
                    deep in the cedar groves.
                    wet brush, tin pants, snoose
Split-shake roof barns
        over berryfields
            white birch chickencoop

Put up in Dick Meigs cabin
                out behind the house—
Coffeecan, PA tin, rags, dirty cups,
Kindling fell behind the stove
                            miceshit
            old magazines,

                    winter's coming in the mountains
                    shut down the show
                    the punks go back to school
                    & the rest hit the road

        strawberries picked, shakeblanks split
        fires all out and the packstrings brought
        down to the valleys
                    set to graze

Gray wharves and hacksaw gothic homes
Shingle mills and stump farms
                            overgrown.

Fifty drunk Indians   *Mt. Vernon*
Sleep in the bus station
Strawberry pickers speaking Kwakiutl
                    turn at Burlington for Skagit
                                    & Ross Dam

        under appletrees by the river
        banks of junkd cars

            B. C. drivers give hitch-hikers rides

"The sheriff's posse stood in double rows   *Everett*
        flogged the naked Wobblies down
        with stalks of Devil's Club
        & run them out of town"

While shingle-weavers lost their fingers
        in the tricky feed and take
            of double saws.

Dried, shrimp   *Seattle*
            smoked,   salmon
        —before the war old indian came
& sold us hard-smoked Chinook
From his truck-bed model T
                    Lake City,

        waste of trees & topsoil, beast, herb,
        edible roots, Indian field-farms & white men
        dances   washed, leached, burnt out
        Minds blunt, ug! talk twisted

A night of the long poem
and the mined guitar . . .
"Forming the new society
within the shell of the old"
        mess of tincan camps and littered roads

The Highway passes straight through
                    every town
At Matsons washing blujeans
            hills and saltwater
                    ack, the woodsmoke in my brain

High Olympics—can't go there again

        East Marginal Way the hitch-hike zone
        Boeing down across Duwamish slough
& angle out
        & on.

Night rain wet concrete headlights
                    blind   *Tacoma*

    Salt air/   Bulk cargo/   Steam cycle

            AIR REDUCTION

        eating peanuts I don't give a damn
        if anybody ever stops   I'll walk
        to San Francisco   what the hell

                "that's where you're going?
                "why you got that pack?

Well man I just don't feel right
Without something on my back

      & this character in milkman overalls
      "I have to come out here
      every onct in a while, there's a guy
      blows me here"

              way out of town.

Stayed in Olympia with Dick Meigs
   —this was a different year & he had moved—
sleep on a cot in the back yard
half the night watch falling stars

These guys got babies now
         drink beer, come back from wars
      "I'd like to save up all my money
      get a big new car, go down to Reno
      & latch onto one of those rich girls—
      I'd fix their little ass"—nineteen yr old
      N. Dakota boy fixing to get married next month
To Centralia in a purple ford.

        carstruck dead doe
        by the Skookumchuck river

Fat man in a Chevrolet
        wants to go back to L.A.
        "too damnd poor now"
Airbrakes on the log trucks hiss and whine
Stand in the dark by the stoplight.
        big fat cars tool by

Drink coffee, drink more coffee
                            brush teeth back of Shell
        hot shoes
                    stay on the rightside of that
                            yellow line

Marys Corner, turn for Mt. Rainier
        —once caught a ride at night for Portland here
Five Mexicans, ask me "chip in on the gas"
        I never was more broke & down.
        got fired that day by the USA
        (the District Ranger up at Packwood
        thought the wobblies had been dead for
                                    forty years
        but the FBI smelled treason
                        —my red beard)

That Waco Texas boy
        took A. G. & me through miles of snow
        had a chest of logger gear
        at the home of an Indian girl
        in Kelso, hadn't seen since Fifty-four

Toledo, Castle Rock, free way
            four lane
        no stoplights & no crossings, only cars
        & people walking, old hitch-hikers
        break the law. How do I know.
                        the state cop
                            told me so.

Come a dozen times into
                    Portland
        on the bum or
                    hasty lover
            late   at   night

III

Portland

dust kicking up behind the trucks—night rides—
who waits in the coffee stop
                                  night highway 99

    Sokei-an met an old man on the banks of the
    Columbia river growing potatoes & living all alone,
    Sokei-an asked him the reason why he lived there,
    he said

    Boy, no one ever asked me the reason why.
    I like to be alone.
    I am an old man.
    I have forgotten how to speak human words.

All night freezing
    in the back of a truck
  dawn at Smith river
    battering on in loggers pickups
               prunes for lunch
The next night, Siuslaw.

Portland sawdust   down town
Buttermilk corner,   all you want for a nickel
  (now a dime)
         —Sujata gave Gautama
                buttermilk,
    (No doubt! says Sokei-an, that's all it was
              plain buttermilk.)

rim of mountains. pulp bark chewd snag
                              papermill
    tugboom in the river
    —used to lean on bridgerails
    dreaming up eruptions and quakes—

Slept under Juniper in the Siskiyou   (Yreka)
    a sleeping bag, a foot of snow
    black rolled umbrella
    ice slick asphalt

Caught a ride the only car come by
    at seven in the morning
    chewing froze salami

Riding with a passed-out LA whore
    glove compartment full of booze,
    the driver a rider, nobody cowboy,
    sometime hood,
Like me picked up to drive,
    & drive the blues away.
              we drank to Portland
                    & we treated that girl good.

I split my last two bucks with him in town
    went out to Carol & Billy's in the woods.

    —foggy morning in Newport
    housetrailers
          under the fir.

An old book on Japan at the Goodwill
    unfurld umbrella in the sailing snow
       sat back in black wood
              barber college
         chair, a shave
On Second Street in Portland
           what elegance.   What a life.

       bust my belly with a quart of
               buttermilk
    & five dry heels of French bread
    from the market cheap
           clean shaved, dry feet,

We're on our way
        man
           out of town
Go hitching down that
        highway ninety-nine.

IV

Oil-pump broken, motor burning out   *Salem*

Ex-logger selling skidder cable
    wants to get to San Francisco,
    fed and drunk   *Eugene*

Guy just back from Alaska—don't like
    the States, there's too much law   *Sutherlin*

A woman with a kid & two bales of hay.   *Roseburg*

18

Sawmill worker, young guy thinking of
  going to Eureka for redwood logging
  later in the year   *Dillard*

Two Assembly of God Pentecostal boys in
  a Holy Roller High School. One had
          spoken in
              tongues.   *Canyonville*

LASME   Los-Angeles—Seattle Motor Express

      place on highway 20:   LITTLE ELK
                              badger & badger

South of Yoncalla burn the engine
                  run out of oil

Yaquina fishdocks
              candlefish & perch
              slant-faced woman fishing
          tuna stacked like cordwood
          the once-glimpsed-into door
                      company freezer shed
              a sick old seagull settles
              down to die.
              the ordinary, casual, ruffle of the
                      tail & wings.
(Six great highways; so far only one)

      freshwater creeks on the beach sand
              at Kalaloch I caught a bag of water
      at Agate Beach
              made a diversion with my toe

19

Jumpoff Joe Creek &
    a man carrying nothing, walking sort of
    stiff-legged along, blue jeans & denim jacket,
    wrinkled face, just north of
    Louse Creek

      —Abandon really means it
      —the network womb stretched loose all
                          things slip
            through

Dreaming on a bench under newspapers
I woke covered over with Rhododendron blooms
Alone in a State Park in Oregon.

V

    "I had a girl in Oakland who worked
    for a doctor, she was a nurse, she let him
    eat her. She died of tuberculosis   *Grants*
    & I drove back that night   *Pass*
                to Portland
    non stop, crying all the way."

    "I picked up a young mother with two
    children once, their house had just
                    burned down"
    "I picked up an Italian tree-surgeon
    in Port Angeles once, he had all his
    saws and tools all screwed & bolted on
            a beat up bike"

Oxyoke, Wolf Creek,

A guy coming off a five-day binge, to   *Phoenix*

An ex-bartender from Lebanon, to   *Redding*

Man & wife on a drinking spree, to   *Anderson*

Snow on the pines & firs around Lake Shasta
    —Chinese scene of winter hills & trees
    us "little travellers" in the bitter cold

        six-lane highway slash & DC twelves
       bridge building   squat earth-movers
    —yellow bugs

        I speak for hawks.

The road that's followed goes forever;
In half a minute crossed and left behind.

Out of the snow and into red-dirt plains

        blossoming plums

Each time you go that road it gets more straight
   curves across the mountains lost in fill
      towns you had to slow down all four lane
        Azalea, Myrtle Creek
        WATCH OUT FOR DEER

At Project City Indian hitcher
Standing under single tarpole lamp
     nobody stopped
        Ginsberg & I walked
        four miles & camped by an oak fire
        left by the road crew

Going to San Francisco
Yeah San Francisco
Yeah we came from Seattle
Even farther north
Yeah we been working in the mountains
    in the Spring
    in the Autumn
           always go this highway ninety-nine—

"I was working in a mill three weeks there
then it burned down & the guy didn't even
pay us off—but I can do anything—
I'll go to San Francisco—tend bar"

Standing in the night.
In the world-end winds
By the overpass bridge

      Junction US 40 and Highway Ninety-nine

Trucks, trucks,   roll by
Kicking up dust—dead flowers—

Sixteen speeds forward
Windows open
Stoppd at the edge of Willows for a bite

        grass shoots on the edge of
        drained rice plains

           —cheap olives—

Where are the Sierras.

            level, dry,
Highway turns west

            miles gone, speed
                            still
            pass through lower hills
            heat dying
                toward Vallejo
    gray on the salt baywater
        brown grass ridges
                    blue mesquite

One leggd Heron in the tideflats

                    State of Cars.

Sailor getting back to ship
            —I'm sick of car exhaust

        City
    gleaming far away

we make it into town tonight
get clean & drink some wine—

    SAN FRANCISCO

        NO
        body
    gives a shit
                man
        who you are or
            whats your car
        there IS no
                        ninety-nine

Hymn to the Goddess San Francisco in Paradise

If you want to live high get high

—NIHIL C.

I

up under the bell skirt
caving over the soil
white legs flashing
　　—amazed to see under their clothes they are
　　　　　naked
　　　this makes them sacred
& more than they are in their own shape
　　　　free.

the wildest cock-blowing
　　gang-fucking foul-tongued
　　　　head chick
　　thus the most so—

II

high town
high　　in the dark　　town
　　　dream　sex　church
　　　YAHWEH　peyote spook
　　　Mary the fish-eyed
　　　　　spotless,
　　　　　lascivious,
vomiting molten gold.

24

san fran sisco
hung over & swing down
            dancers on water
      oil slick glide
      shaman longshoremen
      magical strikes—
howls of the guardians rise from the waterfront.
—state line beauties those switcher engines
            leading waggons
warehouz of jewels and fresh fur

car leans
      on its downhill springs
                  parked on mountainsides.
white minarets in the night
      demon fog chaos.
bison stroll on the grass.
      languid and elegant, fucking while standing
                  young couples in silk
                        make-up on.

crystal towers   gleam for a hundred miles
                  poison oak hedges, walld child garden
& the ring mountains holding a cool
            basin of pure evening fog
            strained thru the bridge
            gold and orange,
beams of cars wiser than drivers
      stream across promenades, causeways
            incensed exhaust.

smiling the City Hall Altar to Heaven
      they serve up the cock   tail,
there is higher than nature in city
            it spins in the sky.

quenching the blue flame
tasting the tea brought from China
cracking the fresh duck egg on white plate

passed out the gates of our chambers
over the clear miles, ships.
forever such ecstasy
     wealth & such beauty
      we live in the sign of Good Will . . .
(the white-robed saint trim my locks for
     a paltry sum . . . life is
     like free)
rolling lawns clippt and the smell of gum tree.
boiled crab from a saltwater vat.
              rhine wine.
bison and elk of Chrysopylae
eels in those rocks in the wave
olive oil, garlic, soy, hard cheese.

Devas of small merit in Jambudvipa
Plucking sour berries to eat:
shall ascend to an eminence,
scanning the scene
    fog in
    from the Farallones
long ship low   far below
   sliding under the bridge
   bright white.   red-lead.
          —blue of the sea.
   on that ship is me.

IV

—smilers all on the nod nap on cots
but the slither   & breakfree
      tosst slipper up on the toe
        & the white thighs open
          the flesh of the wet flower
        LAW
crossed eyes gleam   *come*
      flowery prints and
      yellow kettles in a row
      breast weight swelld down

kind chairmen smile around,
generals and presidents swallow
        hoping   they too   can come . . .
  THERE IS NO WAY

     turn back dead tourist
      drop your crumb your funny passport
—fall back richer spenders
     think you make with wild teenager
        on hard forever
       crust in jewel
       —you are too old.
the san francisco fake front strip tease
phony, sweaty,
last a minute and they stink and die

THIS LAND IS FOR THE HIGH
    & love is for ten thousand years.
        (damnd square climbers give me pains)
them wilty blossoms on her sweaty brow—
     the flute and lute and drums

policecars sireen down on Fillmore
fog clears back away
the police close in
    & shoot the loose
& clouds are slipping by

& hide it in your pockets.

It all becomes plain sky.

The Market

heart of the city
        down   town.
the country   side.

John Muir.   up before dawn
packing pears in the best boxes
       beat out the others—to Market
           the Crystal Palace
on the morning milk-run train.

me, milk bottles by bike
guernsey milk, six percent butterfat
raw and left to rise natural
               ten cents a quart
slipped on the ice turning
          in to a driveway
   and broke all nine bottles.
 when we had cows.
     a feathery hemlock out back
     by manure pile where
           one cow once
    lay with milkfever   transfusions
   & worries until the vet come
we do this still dark in the morning—

to town on high thin-wheeled carts.
squat on the boxtop stall.
papayas   banana   slicd fish   grated ginger

fruit for fish, meat for flowers
french bread for ladle
steamer, tea giant
rough glaze earthware
—for brass shrine bowls.

push through fish
bound pullets lay on their sides
wet slab
watch us with glimmering eye
slosh water.
a carrot, a lettuce.   a ball of cookd noodle.
beggars hang by the flower stall
give them all some

strong women.   dirt from the hills
in her nails.

valley thatch houses
palmgroves for hedges
ricefield and thrasher
to white rice
dongs and piastre
to market, the
changes, how much
is our change:

II

seventy-five feet hoed rows equals
one hour explaining power steering
equals two big crayfish =
all the buttermilk you can drink
= twelve pounds cauliflower

= five cartons greek olives = hitch-hiking
              from Ogden Utah to Burns Oregon
= aspirin, iodine, and bandages
= a lay in Naples = beef
= lamb ribs   = Patna
                   long grain rice, eight pounds
equals two kilogram soybeans = a boxwood
                                    geisha comb.
equals the whole family at the movies
equals whipping dirty clothes on rocks
    three days, some Indian river
= piecing off beggars two weeks
= bootlace and shoelace
        equals one gross inflatable
        plastic pillows
= a large box of petit-fours, chou-crêmes—
        barley-threshing
    mangoes, apples, custard apples, raspberries
= picking three flats strawberries
= a christmas tree = a taxi ride
carrots, daikon, eggplant, greenpeppers,
oregano   white   goat   cheese
        = a fresh-eyed bonito, live clams.
a swordfish
a salmon
    a handful of silvery smelt in the pocket;
        whiskey in cars.   out late after dates.
        old folks   eating cake   in secret
        breastmilk enough.
                     if the belly be fed—

& wash-down.   hose off aisles
reach under fruitstands
        green gross rack
                meat scum on chop blocks
                bloody butcher concrete floor
        old knives sharpened down to scalpels
                brown wrap paper rolls, stiff
                        push-broom back
wet spilld food
                when the market is closed
                        the cleanup comes
                                equals

a billygoat pushing through people
stinking and grabbing a cabbage
arrogant, tough,
he took it—they let him—
Katmandu—the market

I have a man seventy paise
in return for a clay pot
of curds
was it worth it?
how can I tell

                        III

they eat feces
        in the dark
        on stone floors.
one legged animals, hopping cows
        limping dogs   blind cats

crunching garbage in the market
  broken fingers
     cabbage
  head on the ground.

who has young face.
  open pit eyes
between the bullock carts and people
  head pivot with the footsteps
       passing by
dark scrotum spilld on the street
  penis laid by his thigh
     torso
turns with the sun

I came to buy
  a few bananas by the ganges
   while waiting for my wife.

Journeys

I

Genji caught a gray bird, fluttering. It
was wounded, so I hit it with a coal shovel.
It stiffened, grew straight and symmetrical,
and began to increase in size. I took it by
the head with both hands and held it as it
swelled, turning the head from side to side.
It turned into a woman, and I was embracing
her. We walked down a dim-lighted stairway
holding hands, walking more and more swiftly
through an enormous maze, all underground.
Occasionally we touched surface, and redescended.
As we walked I kept a chart of our route in
mind—but it became increasingly complex—and
just when we reached the point where I was
about to lose my grasp of it, the woman trans-
ferred a piece of fresh-tasting apple from her
mouth to mine. Then I woke.

II

Through deep forests to the coast,
and stood on a white sandspit looking in:
over lowland swamps and prairies
where no man had ever been
to a chill view of the Olympics, in a chill clear wind.

III

We moved across dark stony ground to the great
wall: hundreds of feet high. What was beyond
it, cows?—then a thing began to rise
up from behind.

I shot my arrows, shot arrows at it, but it came—
until we turned and ran, "It's too big to
fight"—the rising thing a quarter mile across—
it was the flaming, pulsing sun. We fled and
stumbled on the bright lit plain.

IV

Where were we—
A girl in a red skirt, high heels,
going up the stairs before me in a made-over barn.
White-wash peeling, we lived together in the loft,
on cool bare boards.
—lemme tell you something kid—
　　　　back in 1910.

V

Walking a dusty road through plowed-up fields
at forest-fire time—the fir tree hills dry,
smoke of the far fires blurred the air—
& passed on into woods, along a pond,
beneath a big red cedar,
to a bank of blinding blue wild flowers
and thick green grass on levelled ground
of hillside where our old house used to stand.
I saw the footings damp and tangled,
and thought my father was in jail,
and wondered why my mother never died,
and thought I ought to bring my sister back.

VI

High up in a yellow-gold
dry range of mountains—

brushy, rocky, cactussy hills
slowly hiking down—finally can see below,
a sea of clouds.

Lower down, always moving slowly over the
dry ground descending, can see through breaks
in the clouds: flat land.
Damp green level ricefields, farm houses,
at last to feel the heat and damp.

Descending to this humid, clouded, level world:
now I have come to the LOWLANDS.

VII

Underground building chambers clogged with refuse heaps
discarded furniture, slag, old nails,
rotting plaster, faint wisps—antique newspapers
rattle in the winds that come forever down the hall.
ladders
passing, climbing, and stopping, on from door to door.
one tiny light bulb left still burning
                    —now the last—
locked *inside* is hell.
Movies going, men milling round the posters
                in shreds
                the movie always running
—we all head in here somewhere;

—years just looking for the bathrooms.
Huge and filthy, with strange-shaped toilets full of shit.
Dried shit all around, smeared across the walls of the
adjoining room,
and a vast hat rack.

36

VIII

With Lew rode in a bus over the mountains—
rutted roads along the coast of Washington
through groves of redwood. Sitting in the
back of an almost-empty bus,
talking and riding through.
Yellow leaves fluttering down. Passing
through tiny towns at times. Damp cabins
set in dark groves of trees.
Beaches with estuaries and sandbars. I brought
a woman here once long ago,
but passed on through too quick.

IX

We were following a long river into the mountains.
Finally we rounded a ridge and could see deeper in—
the farther peaks stony and barren, a few alpine
trees.
Ko-san and I stood on a point by a cliff, over a
rock-walled canyon. Ko said, "Now we have come to
where we die." I asked him, what's that up there,
then—meaning the further mountains.
"That's the world after death." I thought it looked
just like the land we'd been travelling, and couldn't
see why we should have to die.
Ko grabbed me and pulled me over the cliff—
both of us falling. I hit and I was dead. I saw
my body for a while, then it was gone. Ko was
there too. We were at the bottom of the gorge.
We started drifting up the canyon, "This is the
way to the back country."

The Blue Sky

"Eastward from here,
    beyond Buddha-worlds ten times as
    numerous as the sands of the Ganges
there is a world called
        PURE AS LAPIS LAZULI
its Buddha is called Master of Healing,
        AZURE RADIANCE TATHAGATA"

    it would take you twelve thousand summer vacations
    driving a car due east all day every day
    to reach the edge of the Lapis Lazuli realm of
    Medicine Old Man Buddha—
    East. Old Man Realm
    East across the sea, yellow sand land
    Coyote old man land
    Silver, and stone blue

Blue   blāew, bright   flāuus   flamen, brāhman

Sky.   skȳ   scūwo   "shadow"
              Sanskrit skutās   "covered"
              skewed (pied)
                    skewbald (. . ."Stewball")
              skybald / Piebald
                    Horse with lightning feet, a mane like
                    distant rain, the Turquoise horse,
                    a black star for an eye
                    white shell teeth

38

Pony that feeds on the pollen of flowers
may he
make thee whole.

Heal.   hail   whole   (khailaz . . . kail . . . koil I.E.r)

Namo bhagavate bhaishajyaguru-vaidurya-
prabharajaya tathagata arhate samyak
sambuddhaya tadyatha *om* bhaishajye
bhaishajye bhaishajya samudgate
svāhā.

"I honour the Lord, the Master of Healing,
shining like lapis lazuli, the king, the
Tathagata, the Saint, the perfectly enlightened
one, saying *OM* TO THE HEALING
TO THE HEALING   TO THE HEALER
HAIL!
svāhā.

Shades of blue through the day

T'u chüeh   a border tribe near China
Türc
Turquoise: a hydrous phosphate of aluminum
a little copper
a little iron—

Whole, Whole, Make Whole!

39

Blue Land Flaming Stone–
Man
      Eastward—
            sodium, aluminum, calcium, sulfur.

In the reign of the Emperor Nimmyō
when Ono-no-Komachi the strange girl poet
was seventeen, she set out looking for her father
who had become a Buddhist Wanderer. She took ill
on her journey, and sick in bed one night saw

AZURE RADIANCE THUS-COME MEDICINE MASTER

in a dream. He told her she would find a hotsprings
on the bank of the Azuma river in the Bandai mountains
that would cure her; and she'd meet her father there.

      "Enchantment as strange as
      the Blue up above"   my rose of San Antone

Tibetans believe that Goddesses have Lapis Lazuli hair.

Azure.   O.F. azur
            Arabic lāzaward
            Persian lāzhward   "lapis lazuli"

—blue bead charms against the evil eye—

(*Hemp.* ". . . Cheremiss and Zyrjän word . . . these two languages
    being Finno-Ugric—
    a wandering culture word
    of wide diffusion.")

Tim and Kim and Don and I were talking about
what an awful authoritarian garb Doctors
and Nurses wear, really, how spooky it is.
"What *should* they wear?"

—"Masks and Feathers!"

Ramana Maharshi Dream

I was working as a wood cutter by a crossroads—Ko-san
was working with me—we were sawing and splitting the
firewood. An old man came up the lane alongside a mud
wall—he shouted a little scolding at some Zen monks who
were piling slash by the edge of the woods. He came over
and chatted with us, a grizzled face—neither eastern or
western; or both. He had a glass of buttermilk in his
hand. I asked him "Where'd you get that buttermilk?"
I'd been looking all over for buttermilk. He said,
"At the O K Dairy, right where you leave town."

41

Medicine.   medēri   Indo European   me–
         "to measure"
    "MAYA"   Goddess   illusion-wisdom   fishing net

Herba.   (some pre-latin rustic word . . .)

Lazuli   sodium, aluminum, calcium, sulfur, silicon;
    sky blue
    right in the rocks too—
    Lazuli Bunting
    sea-blue
    hazy-hills blue
    huckleberry, cobalt
    medicine-bottle
    blue.

Celestial   arched cover . . . kam

Heaven   heman . . . kam

    [*comrade:*   under the same sky/tent/curve]
      Kamarā, Avestan, a girdle kam,   a bent curved bow

        Kāma, God of Lust   "Son of Maya"
              "Bow of Flowers"

:Shakyamuni would then be the lord of the present
world of sorrow; Bhaishajyaguru / Yao-shih Fo /

Yakushi; "Old Man Medicine Buddha" the lord of the
Lost Paradise.

Glory of morning,
        pearly gates, the
                heavenly bue.

Thinking on Amitabha in the setting sun,
        his western paradise—
        impurities flow out away, to west,
        behind us, *rolling*

        planet ball forward turns into the "east"
        is rising,
        azure,
        two thousand light years ahead

        Great Medicine Master;
        land of blue.

        The Blue Sky

        The Blue Sky

        The Blue Sky

        is the land of

OLD MAN MEDICINE BUDDHA

where the Eagle
that Flies out of Sight

flies.